EGMONT

We bring stories to life

First published in Great Britain 2008
by Egmont UK Limited
239 Kensington High Street, London W8 6SA
Illustrations by Robin Davies.
© 2008 HIT Entertainment Limited and Keith Chapman.
All rights reserved. The Bob the Builder name and character,
related characters and the Bob figure and riveted logo are
trademarks of HIT Entertainment Limited. Reg. U.S. Pat.
& TM. Off. and in the UK and other countries.

ISBN 978 1 4052 3725 3
1 3 5 7 9 10 8 6 4 2
Printed in Singapore

palm tree

pear

melon

bananas

pineapple

chicks

Farmer
Pickles

grapes

hay bales

sheep

Mr Beasley

Cassia

Carlo

ducklings

ducks

Bob's Workshop

Dizzy

door

ladder

fire extinguisher

Wendy

bucket

saw

work bench

bricks

toolbox

sawdust

wood

paint pot

paint brush

set square

hacksaw

pliers

drill

hard hat

poster

clipboard

hammer

mallet

spanner

lathe

chisel

Pilchard

cupboard

trowel

Bob

torch

screwdriver

screws

pencil

notebook

12

3

ruler

nails

counter top

tape
measure

Can you find . . .

a cake?

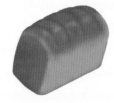

bread loaves?

a toy train?

some teddy bears?

In the General Store

buns

shelves

bread loaves

mop

jam tarts

cake

Mrs Bentley

cheese

pizza

jam

yoghurt

chicken

sausages

pork pies

eggs

wool

wellington
boots

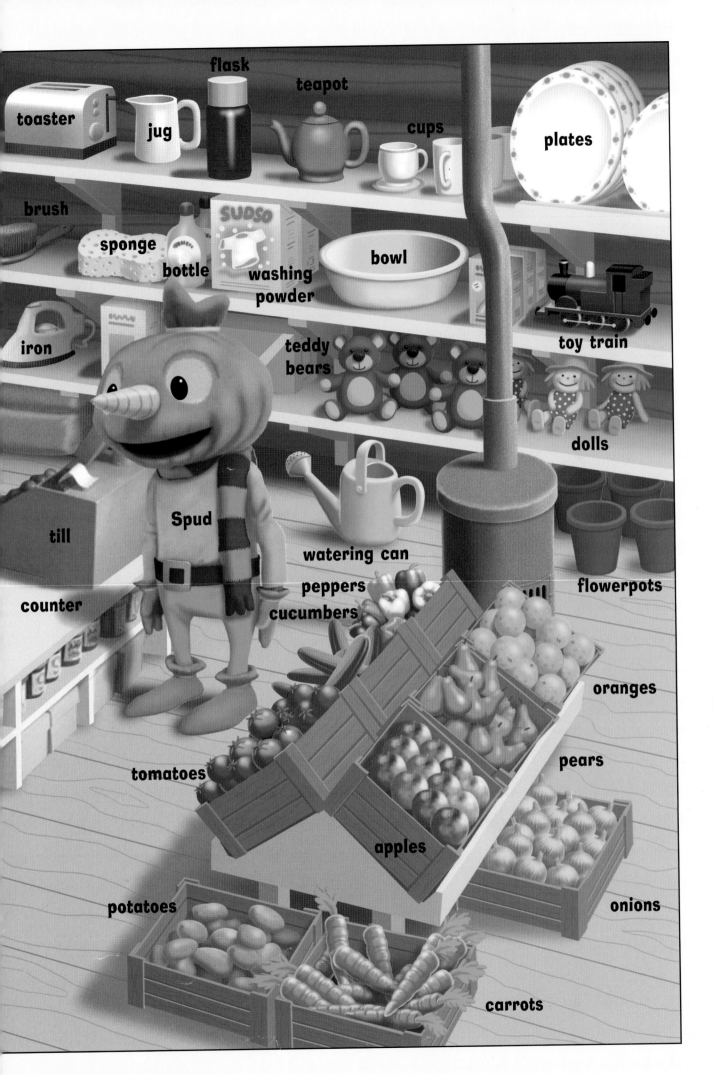

toaster

flask

jug

teapot

cups

plates

brush

sponge

bottle

SUDSO

washing powder

bowl

toy train

iron

teddy bears

dolls

Spud

watering can

flowerpots

till

counter

peppers

cucumbers

oranges

tomatoes

pears

apples

onions

potatoes

carrots

a teapot?

some plates?

a brush?

a pizza?

wellington boots?

At the Beach

lighthouse

sun

cliffs

umbrella

seagull

rocks

deckchair

Saffron

beach huts

Scruffty

Frisbee

water

Wendy

sun lotion

Bob

bag

beach towel

pebbles

shells

seaweed

At the Playground

Roley

Bird

squirrels

Carlo

Marjorie

Sunny

Mrs Sabatini

see-saw

Cassia

butterfly

slide

crow

Spud

toy plane

Pilchard

rope bridge

skipping rope

Saffron

basketball

ramp

cricket bat

badminton racket
and shuttlecock

cricket ball

In the Countryside

squirrel

butterfly

gate

fox

Ela Stevenson

sheep

bicycle

bumblebee

eggs

bird's nest

mole

mole hill

sunflowers

Spud's Bedroom

toy mouse

poster

lamp

picture frame

hammock bed

Spud

mug

chest of drawers

teddy bear

handkerchief

cake

book

blanket

marbles

socks

scarf

rug

skateboard

kite

toy plane

mirror

tennis racket

television

plant

suitcase

box

radio

drumstick

drum

broom

stool

toy car

hay bale

trumpet

football   jigsaw pieces

Sunflower Valley Shapes!

Can you find . . .

a diamond?

a star?

a triangle?

roof

flask

biscuits

mug

Roley

crate

cloud

tree

trowel

Bob

Wendy

wall

a circle?

a heart?

a square?

a rectangle?

At the Pond

Can you find . . .

a dragonfly?

bullrushes?

this duck?

brambles

bushes

otter

frog

Benny

Mr Beasley

fishing rod

Pilchard

oar   rowing boat

float

fish

pond

trees

dragonfly

Bob

rope

Wendy

bread

ducks

lilypads

bullrushes

lizard

an otter?

a lizard?

this fish?

a frog?

Colourful Sunflower Valley!

Scoop is yellow.

What other yellow things do you know?

Benny is pink.

What other pink things do you know?

Bob's coat is brown.

What other brown things do you know?

Roley is green.

What other green things do you know?

Lofty is blue.

What other blue things
do you know?

Muck is red.

What other red things
do you know?

Dizzy is orange.

What other orange things
do you know?

Wendy's clothes are purple.

What other purple things
do you know?

Let's Go Camping!

Birdie

shelter

flag

tent

Bob

flask

squirrels

Wendy

Mrs Bentley

Mr Bentley

water trough

otters

toolbox

leaves

bird table

Birdie's chicks

ropes

ladder

bird food

Dizzy

Mr and Mrs Bentley are camping in Sunflower Valley! They love waking up in their tent and seeing the countryside around them.

Bob and his team have built a special bird table nearby. Birdie and her chicks and lots of squirrels and otters are enjoying playing on it.

Today, Bob is topping up the water trough. He's really pleased to see the birds and animals having so much fun.

Summer

Winter

snow

chimney

star

Zoomer

lights

icicles

Sunny

hat

Saffron

gloves

sledge

baubles

snowball

robin

Scoop

Christmas
tree

Spud

Bob

scarf

snowman

spade

coat

snow plough

Days of the Week

Monday

On Monday, Farmer Pickles asks Bob to build a storage shelter for him. It has to be ready for the grand opening of his factory on Sunday.

Tuesday

Early on Tuesday morning, Bob and the team get to work on building the bottle depot to store Farmer Pickles' bottles of sunflower oil.

Wednesday

On Wednesday, Sumsy comes to the factory. She gets to work with Scoop, lifting and stacking the boxes for delivery to the depot.

Thursday

On Thursday, disaster strikes! Some boxes of oil are knocked over and the bottles break. It takes a long time to clean up the mess.

Friday

By Friday, Bob has finished building the bottle depot. Farmer Pickles asks Sumsy and Scoop to deliver all the boxes of oil to the depot.

Saturday

On Saturday, Sumsy and Scoop are busy, travelling backwards and forwards, carrying boxes of oil. Soon they've finished the job.

Sunday

On Sunday, it's the Grand Opening Day. Farmer Pickles thanks the team for their help, as he declares the Sunflower Factory open!

At the Café

moon

bats

Bird

Mrs Sabatini

Spud

Roley

cake

pancakes

Farmer Pickles

Scruffty

Tell the Time with Bob

At 7 o'clock, Bob meets Wendy.
They are building the Dome today!

At 8 o'clock, Lofty, Scoop, Roley,
Muck and Dizzy arrive to help them.

By 9 o'clock, the foundations are laid.
Then Dizzy pours in the concrete.

At 10 o'clock, the Dome's wooden panels
and triangular windows arrive.

By 11 o'clock, Lofty has helped put the first section of windows on the Dome.

At 12 o'clock, Wendy has lunch with Mr and Mrs Bentley. They've invited everyone to the Dome opening party that night.

At 1 o'clock, Wendy asks Scrambler to take Scruffty for a run in the valley.

By 2 o'clock, they're racing through muddy puddles – splash!

Tell the Time with Bob

At 3 o'clock, Wendy asks Mr Bentley to fetch balloons for the opening party.

At 4 o'clock, Wendy calls Roley to flatten the ground before the party.

At 5 o'clock, Roley uses his talkie-talkie to call the other machines to the party.

By 6 o'clock, Wendy wonders if the Dome will be finished in time. Bob promises to get the job done!

At 7 o'clock, the Dome is ready!
Bob celebrates with his friends, before happily going home to bed.